THIS BOOK BELONGS TO:

_____

To my Uncle Marvin, an extraordinary baseball player and all-around great guy whose indomitable spirit should be an inspiration for us all.

— M.E.S

To Marvin, my big brother, my mentor and friend, who didn't just think he was a great baseball player... he knew he was a great baseball player. To our dad, Porter E. Price, who taught Marvin the essentials of playing baseball and to our mother, Mary E. Price, whose loving and caring persona guided Marvin, always.

— G.P.S.

ISBN-13: 978-0692805701

Printed in the United States of America

Open Book Company

I AM A BASEBALL PLAYER

A True Story About Baseball's Youngest Pro

by Maria E. Stimpson & Gloria Price Stimpson

Open Book Company

*W*hen Marvin Daniel Price was three
He knew what he would one day be.
And if you asked him, "Who are you?"
Loud and proud, he'd say to you,

"I'M A BASEBALL PLAYER!"

And it was true.

His dad showed Marvin how to hit
And catch a baseball in his mitt.
He liked to run the bases too
Then tell the world, both me and you,

"I'M A BASEBALL PLAYER!"

And it was true.

When Marvin had measles and could not play
He watched his friends play ball one day.
When they saw Marvin, they called out,
"Umpire our game. Call! Shout!"

So, Marvin said, "Sure, piece-a-cake."
"PLAY BALL!" he called.
"For goodness sake!"

His calls were good. His calls were great.
All from an ump who was barely eight!

Marvin grew big and strong and tall.
A mighty fine player of baseball.

As captain of his high school team
He wore 22 and played like a dream.

He practiced hard. Played the right way.
Just right for the Big League. But then one day…

In Spring of 1946
His father gently said,

"Son, though you play great baseball
There's a rocky road ahead.
It breaks my heart to say to you
All Major League teams are white.
Though they give all kinds of reasons,
We know that it just ain't right.

My son, the Majors aren't for you.
What do you really want to do?"

With a tear in his eye
Marvin could not deny.

"I'M A BASEBALL PLAYER!"

And he wanted to cry.

Mr. Price walked slowly out of the room.
His son might as well have reached for the moon.

Marvin went to Washington Park
Where older boys played until dark.

He got in the game. Played like a pro.
Made it look easy when they threw high or low.

Wide or wild. In the dirt. Round-about.
He caught the ball and tagged runners ***"out."***

Someone special was watching that day.
From the Negro Leagues he came to see them play.

All-Star Jimmie Crutchfield was very impressed.
Marvin, the youngest, was clearly the best!

"Hey, kid. How old are you?" Jimmie asked.
"You play just like a pro."

"Almost 14, sir," Marvin said.
"But I started playing a ***long*** time ago."

"You are a natural," Jimmie said.
"Try out with my team.

The Giants sure could use you ***if*—**
You're as good as you seem.

Go to Comiskey tomorrow and play
Exactly the way you played here today."

When Marvin went to Comiskey Park
The team manager misunderstood.
"Look kid, I don't need a bat boy," he said.
"I need someone who plays really good."

The players on the Giants laughed.
Teasing was all they would do.
"Go home, bat boy," they yelled at him.
"Yo mama is calling you!"

"I'm not a bat boy!" Marvin said.
"I play baseball really good.
Just gimme a chance to try out.
Watch me smash this ball with the wood."

Marvin stepped up to the plate.
Stared the pitcher in the eye.
Took a mighty swing
But the baseball whizzed by.

"STEE-RIKE ONE!"

yelled the umpire.

Marvin gripped the bat.
He gave it his all.
Took another swing.

"STEE-RIKE TWO!"

was the call.

There was no strike three.
Instead, a loud **"CRACK."**

As the ball soared up to the sun
It flew high in the stands
Above happy fans.
Marvin had hit a **HOME RUN!**

The Giants fell silent
Then joined with the crowd.
The fans on their feet
Were cheering out loud.

"Hurray for Marvin!" yelled a small boy.
"He's amazing," said the boy's mother.
"He's a thumper," an old man shouted with joy
As he stood to high-five another.

The team manager smiled at Marvin and said,
"You were right, kid. I misunderstood.
You're not a bat boy you're a ballplayer.
And, heck, you play really good!"

Owner J. B. Martin took his cap from his head.
He gave it to Marvin and then he said,
"Young fella, the Giants want you on our team.
Though you are 13 you play older than you seem.

You can go barnstorming with us on our bus.
From this point on, you are now one of us."

To the fans in the stands
With his cap in his hands
Marvin let out a big **"YA-HOOO!"**

To all who would hear
He yelled loud and clear,

"I AM A BASEBALL PLAYER!"

And it was true!

Authors' Notes

Marvin & Gloria

Marvin at age 13

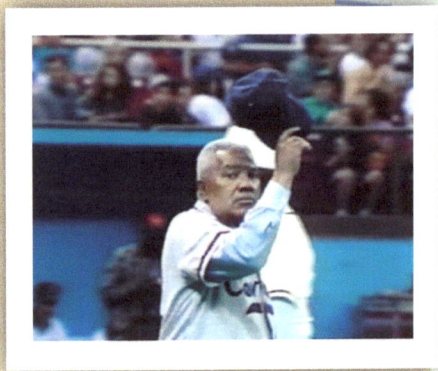

1995 Legends Ceremony

Gloria: When I was growing up in Chicago, my entire household seemed to revolve around baseball. Baseball games were always blaring on the radio during baseball season, no matter which teams were playing. Little did I know then that my big brother would become the youngest professional baseball player ever.

In those days, Major League Baseball was segregated. However, The Negro Leagues welcomed talented players of color – Blacks and Latinos. The Negro Leagues represented the highest attainable professional level of baseball for people of color. The teams drew huge crowds whenever and wherever they went barnstorming.

I remember seeing Marvin play at Comiskey Park when he was a member of the Chicago American Giants. Marvin played in home games but he also travelled with the team when they went barnstorming in the South. Our mom wasn't thrilled with the idea of her 14-year-old son traveling south during the Jim Crow era. Our dad, however, had been acquainted with the Giants. The owner, Dr. J. B. Martin was a dentist and Jimmie Crutchfield and the others were responsible and respectable young men. According to Marvin, Mr. Crutchfield was not just a really nice guy, but also one of the best outfielders to play the game.

Maria: Marvin played in the Negro Leagues for four years, after graduating from high school at 16 years of age. He always said that playing baseball was one of the best experiences of his life. His advice to young baseball players was: work hard to improve your skills; play hard and if anyone ever tells you that you cannot do something, just tell them "watch me!"

Acknowledgements

It takes a village to raise a child and to create a children's book for publication. We would therefore like to acknowledge our village of people who helped tremendously in the creation of this book.

A big thank you to each of our artists —Janvic Victorio, primary illustrator; amazing artist and portraitist, Monica Bucanelli, for capturing our portraits and literally saving the day; Bryce Westervelt for assisting with vignettes and a bookplate; and to cover and book designers, Hammad Khalid and Raphael Albinati for their artistic talent and professionalism.

A very special thank you to author and baseball historian Brent Kelley for recognizing Marvin's place in history so many years ago and to longtime friends, Henry Berry and William Harden, for sharing their priceless memories of Marvin and the good old days. We appreciate each and every one of you!

About the Authors

Maria E. Stimpson is an educational psychologist, award-winning writer and primary author of *I Am A Baseball Player*, based on the true story of her "Uncle Marvin."

Gloria Price Stimpson is a retired teacher, classroom teacher-librarian, mentor, educational consultant and co-author of this true story about her brother, Marvin Daniel Price.

"Although there will always be some debate over who was the youngest to play in the major leagues, if you consider all leagues that were "major" the answer is Marvin Daniel Price."

--Brent Kelley, author
The Negro Leagues Revisited

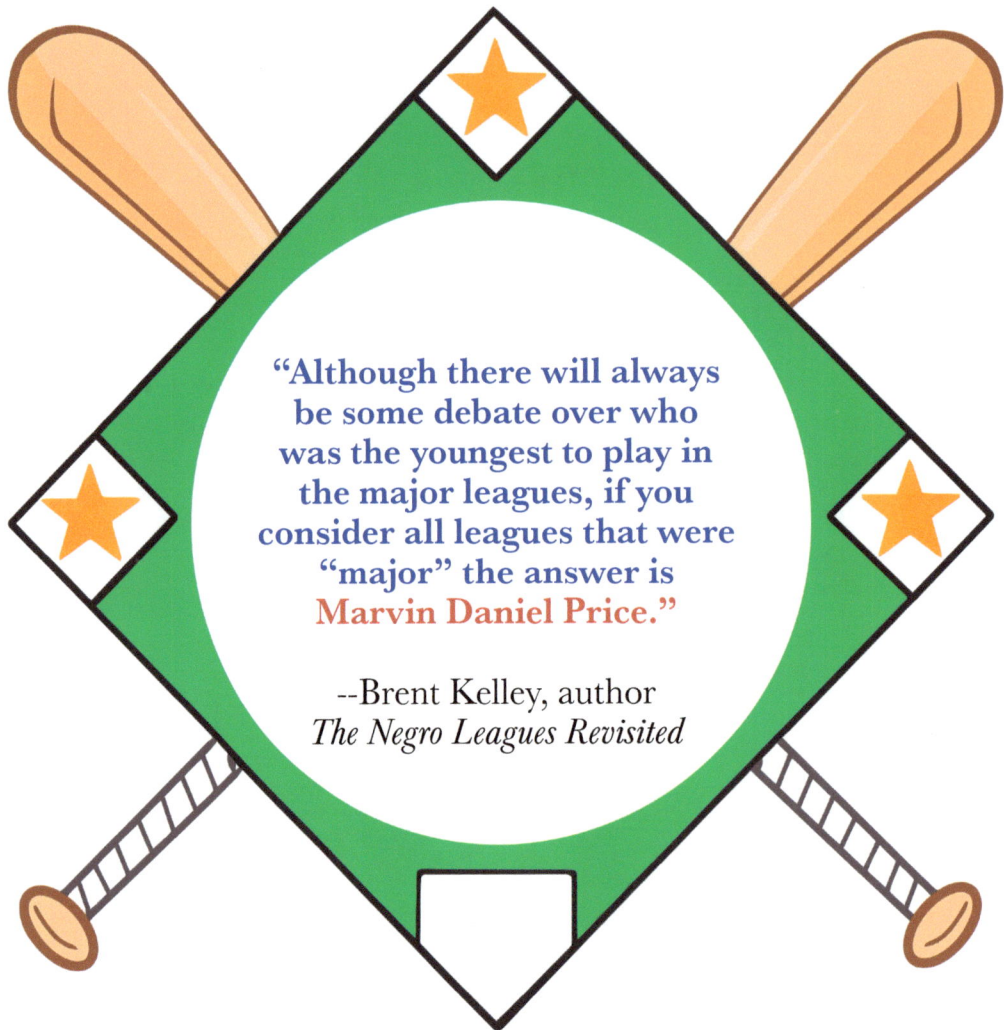

Note: Marvin has been compared to other young baseball professionals who played in only one game. Unlike them, Marvin not only played in home games, but he also travelled with the Chicago American Giants when they went barnstorming. He was barely 14 years old at the time. After graduating from high school at 16, he played baseball professionally from 1949–1952, until he enlisted in the United States Coast Guard.